# Super Noah

Written by: Khayri Johnson

Illustrated by: Markeith Deshun

THIS BOOK IS DEDICATED TO MY BABY BROTHER NOAH,
THE LITTLE HEART WARRIOR THAT CHANGED MY LIFE.

THERE ONCE WAS A SUPER MOM WITH THREE SUPER SONS

AND INSIDE OF HER TUMMY WAS A FOURTH ONE.

BUT DOCTORS WERE SCARED, SOMETHING WAS WRONG,

LITTLE BABY NOAH DID NOT SEEM AS STRONG.

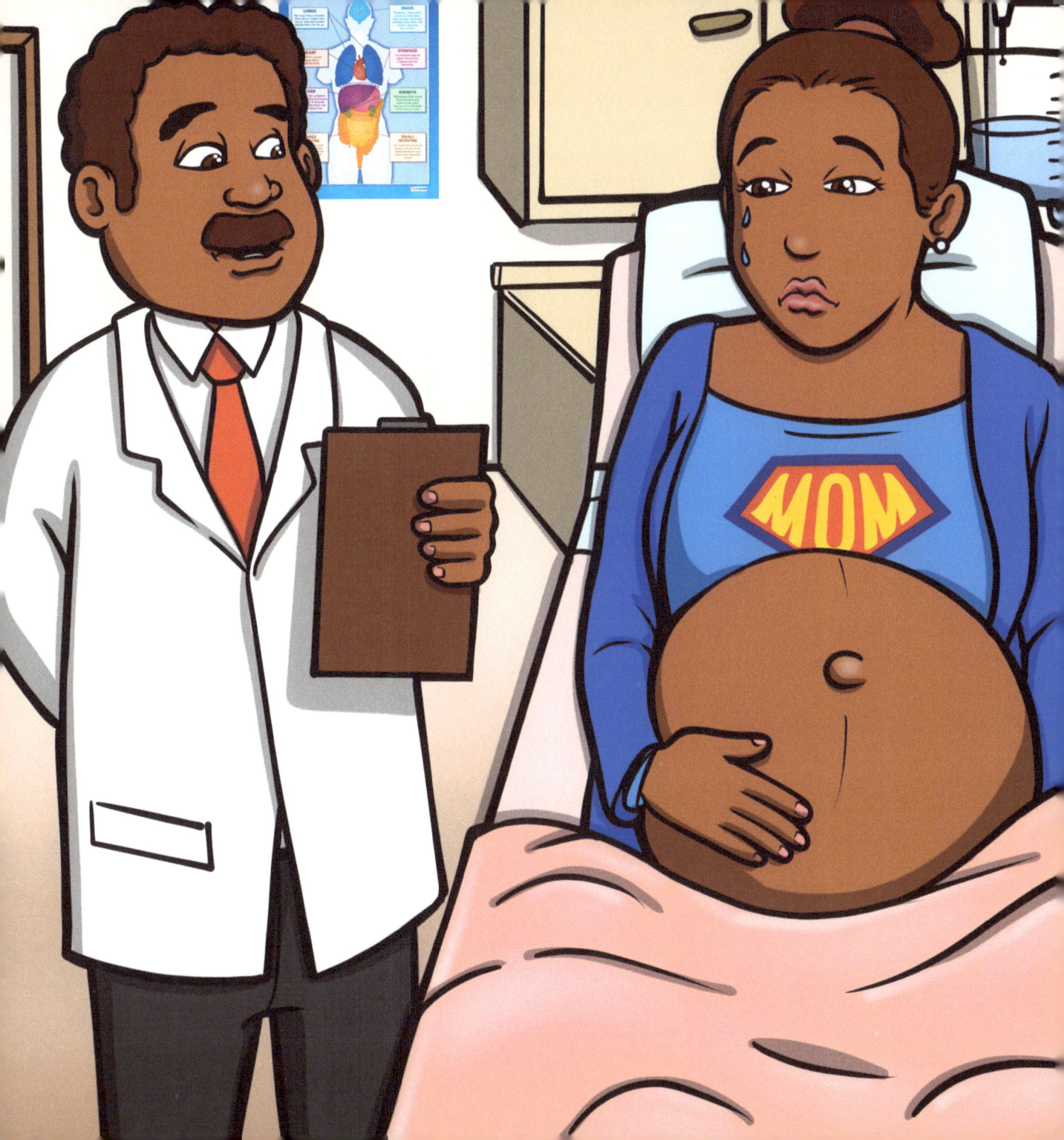

THE MORE DOCTORS FEARED
THE MORE NOAH KNEW

THAT CHANGING PEOPLE'S VIEWS
HE WAS DESTINED TO DO.

AS SUPER MOM PRAYED EVERY SINGLE NIGHT

NOAH BEGAN GROWING STRONGER AND STARTED TO FIGHT.

HE GREW STRONGER AND STRONGER
HIS POWERS HAD FORMED

JANUARY 27TH, A HERO WAS BORN.

HE SMILED AT HIS BIRTH
HE SMILED AT THE WORST

HE SMILED AT PEOPLE ALL OVER THE EARTH.

HE SMILED AT THE BOYS
HE SMILED AT THE GIRLS

HE SMILED UNTIL HIS SMILE
BEGAN CHANGING THE WORLD.

THE WORLD WAS SO FULL OF FROWNS AND THOUGH ONLY A CHILD

THERE WASN'T A PERSON HE COULDN'T MAKE SMILE.

HE HELPED PEOPLE SEE WHAT HE KNEW ALL ALONG

THE FACT HE WAS DIFFERENT IS WHAT MADE HIM STRONG.

EMBRACE WHO YOU ARE
AND REMEMBER THE TRUTH

THERE'S A SUPERHERO IN ME
AND THERE'S A SUPERHERO IN YOU.

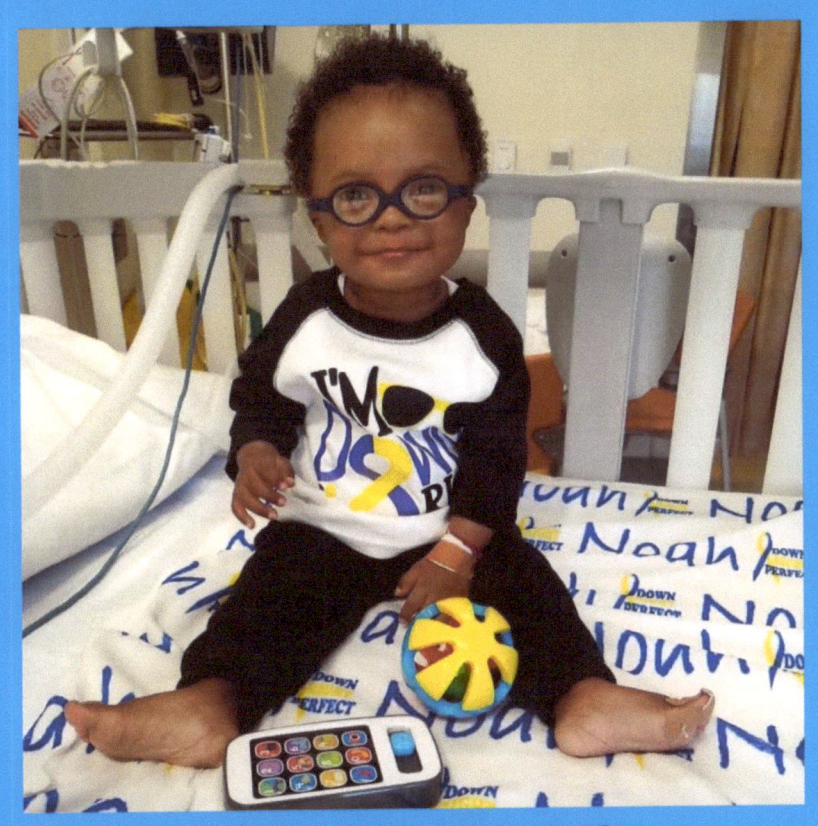

## ABOUT SUPER NOAH JACOB

NOAH JACOB WALKER WAS BORN ON JANUARY 27, 2018 IN BROOKLYN, NEW YORK. HE IS THE YOUNGEST OF FOUR BOYS. NOAH'S MOM WAS INFORMED DURING HER PREGNANCY THAT HER GENETIC TEST RESULTS CAME BACK POSITIVE FOR DOWN SYNDROME. DESPITE THE UNEXPECTED NEWS, SHE DECIDED TO CONTINUE WITH HER PREGNANCY AND BEGAN TO LOVE NOAH MORE AND MORE EACH DAY. UPON HIS ARRIVAL, NOAH WAS DIAGNOSED WITH TRISOMY 21 (DOWN SYNDROME), CONGENITAL HEART DISEASE, MULTICYSTIC KIDNEY DISEASE, PULMONARY HYPERTENSION, AND OBSTRUCTIVE SLEEP APNEA. ALL THESE CONDITIONS DO NOT DEFINE NOAH BECAUSE HE IS ALWAYS HAPPY AND BRINGS JOY TO THOSE AROUND HIM. WITH HIS SPECIAL SUPERPOWERS NOAH OVERCOMES ANY PAIN AND ILLNESS THAT MAY COME HIS WAY. HE IS A LIGHT OF HOPE AND INSPIRATION THAT HAS TOUCHED SO MANY PEOPLE AROUND THE WORLD. THERE IS A SUPERHERO IN ALL OF US AND NOAH IS LIVING PROOF THAT WITH LOVE YOU CAN CONQUER ANYTHING.

## ABOUT THE AUTHOR

KHAYRI JOHNSON'S DEBUT FLASH FICTION CHILDREN'S BOOK, SUPER NOAH, IS A REMARKABLE STORY THAT HE BEGAN CREATING JUST A FEW MONTHS AFTER HIS BABY BROTHER'S 2ND HEART SURGERY. INSPIRED BY NOAH'S STRENGTH AND ABILITY TO CONTINUOUSLY SMILE THROUGH ADVERSITY, KHAYRI WANTED TO TELL NOAH'S STORY IN A WAY THAT WOULD INSPIRE CHILDREN ALL OVER THE WORLD, AS WELL AS THE CHILD IN US ALL. THIS NOW FULL-TIME WRITER, MUSICIAN, AND SUPER BIG BROTHER CALLS THE NEW YORK AREA HOME. HIS WORK CAN BE FOUND ONLINE AT WWW.CHOOSINGNOAH.COM OR ON INSTAGRAM (@BLU.BANE).

## ABOUT THE ILLUSTRATOR

MARKEITH DESHUN IS A FIRST TIME CHILDREN'S BOOK ILLUSTRATOR, LONG TIME ARTIST WHO HAS CREATED COUNTLESS PIECES FROM CARICATURES, POSTERS, BUSINESS LOGOS, MIXTAPE COVERS AND MORE. HE WAS BORN AND RAISED IN COMPTON CALIFORNIA, HE IS A FULL TIME FATHER, THE FOURTH CHILD OF FIVE AND AT AN EARLY AGE HE FOUND A LOVE FOR ART. THROUGHOUT HIS LIFE HE CREATED FINE ART IN MANY DIFFERENT FORMS ON PAPER, SHOES, PANTS, SHIRTS, WALLS AND EVEN MUSIC. MARKEITH LEARNED HOW TO VISUALIZE HIS ART AS WELL AS EXPLORE HIS CREATIVITY ALONG THE WAY. NOW HE'S DESIGNING ART FOR PEOPLE AROUND THE WORLD AND HELPING MANIFEST THEIR VISION TO MAKE IT COME TO LIFE. YOU CAN CONTACT HIM @DESIGNBYDESHUN

# HELPFUL RESOURCES

GLOBAL DOWN SYNDROME FOUNDATION (WWW.GLOBALDOWNSYNDROME.ORG)

DOWN SYNDROME DIAGNOSIS NETWORK (WWW.DSDIAGNOSIS.ORG)

DOWN SYNDROME PREGNANCY (WWW.DOWNSYNDROMEPREGNANCY.ORG)

NATIONAL ASSOCIATION FOR CHILDREN WITH DOWN SYNDROME (WWW.NACDS.ORG)

GIGI'S PLAYHOUSE (WWW.GIGISPLAYHOUSE.ORG)

JACK'S BASKET (WWW.JACKSBASKET.ORG)

THE CHILDREN'S HEART FOUNDATION (WWW.CHILDRENSHEARTFOUNDATION.ORG)

PEDIATRIC CONGENITAL HEART ASSOCIATION (WWW.CONQUERINGCHD.ORG)

NATIONAL KIDNEY FOUNDATION (WWW.KIDNEY.ORG)

AMERICAN SLEEP APNEA ASSOCIATION (WWW.SLEEPAPNEA.ORG)

NATIONAL SLEEP FOUNDATION (WWW.SLEEPFOUNDATION.ORG)

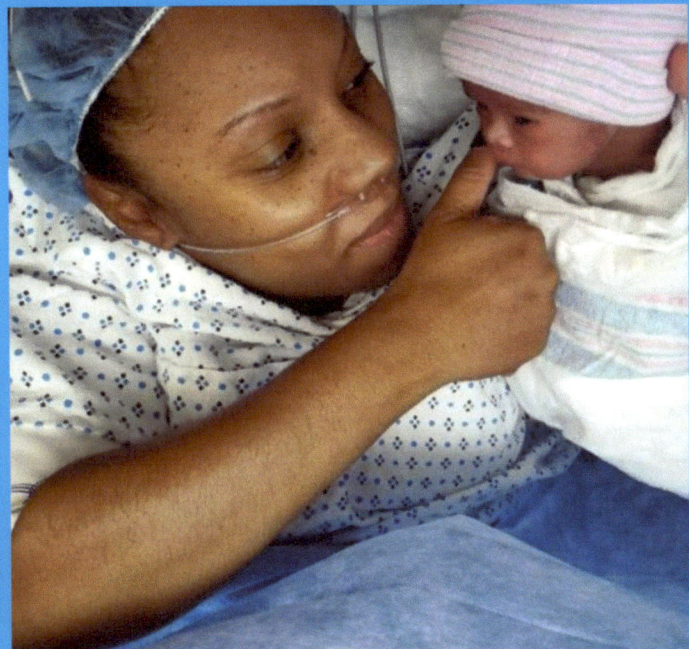

www.ingramcontent.com/pod-product-compliance
Lightning Source LLC
Chambersburg PA
CBHW040729150426
42811CB00063B/1544